A Life Styled by God

A Woman's Workshop on Spiritual Discipline for Weight Control

Pamela E. Snyder

A Life Styled by God: A Woman's Workshop on Spiritual Discipline for Weight Control

This is a Lamplighter Book
Published by the Zondervan Publishing House
1415 Lake Drive, S.E., Grand Rapids, Michigan 49506

Library of Congress Cataloging in Publication Data

Snyder, Pamela E.
A Life styled by God.
(Lamplighter book)
1. Reducing—Psychological aspects. 2. Reducing—Religious aspects—Christianity. 3. Women—Religious life.
RM222.2.S635 1984 613.2'5 84-23451
ISBN 0-310-42791-6

Edited by Lavonne Neff

Printed in the United States of America

85 86 87 88 89 90 / 10 9 8 7 6 5 4 3 2

To my husband, Bob,

a source of daily encouragement

CONTENTS

Preface *15*
Acknowledgments *17*
Introduction *19*
1. Lemon Layer Cake, Anyone? *21*
2. Savor the Fruit *31*
3. Green Lights . . . Caution . . . Stop *39*
4. Footsteps to Follow *50*
5. Unlocking the Chains *57*
6. God's Food, God's Body *66*
7. Made in the Image of God *72*
8. Rest the Horses *79*
9. Do Not Be Led Astray *85*
10. Stressed Out, Bulging Out *95*
11. The Mind Gap *110*
12. Pressing Forward *119*

PREFACE

If you look in the mirror and feel out of place in our "skinny oriented" society, let me assure you that you are not alone: More than 30% of the U.S. population is overweight. Most want to lose weight to improve their appearance. Some are motivated to improve their health. And we Christians have an additional calling—to a lifestyle of self-control.

God's Word shows how self-control can become part of daily life. God's Son gives the ultimate example of self-control. And the Holy Spirit provides the means for change.

As you participate in this study, you will become aware of what you eat and understand what influences your choices. For instance, many of us allow our environment, our friends, and our family to control our choices. Any of these can influence a decision for a second helping of mashed potatoes, a late-night ice cream cone in July, or a piece of your mother-in-law's chocolate chiffon pie. You will discover strategies for changing old habits and finding new choices.

Yet the best strategies are to no avail without God's power and influence on our lives. It is my prayer that as you explore the resources God provides in self-control, you will truly discover a life styled by God.

ACKNOWLEDGMENTS

The behavioral-change techniques used in this book are based on research by a variety of investigators. Albert J. Stunkard, M.D., pioneered using behavioral-change techniques in weight control. He has headed the departments of psychiatry at both Stanford University Medical School and the University of Pennsylvania Medical School. Henry A. Jordan, M.D., and James M. Ferguson, M.D., created specific behavioral self-help tools used in this study.

Special thanks to Karen Bird and Vivian Turnau for reviewing the study, and to Natalie Everett for her typing skills.

INTRODUCTION

Listening to an orchestra can be an exhilarating experience. As you watch the violinist, you may daydream about playing as he does. Yet you cannot learn his skill and achieve his mastery by just sitting there. You must take lessons and practice diligently, going over the same scores over and over again. It is indeed an active process, and you must be willing to pay a price.

So too, you cannot passively read this study and accomplish its goal; you must *do* the exercises step by step to derive benefit. These activities include

diary keeping
self-evaluation questions
"homework" strategies to work on each week
group discussion
accountability to your prayer partner

Not all the strategies given here will apply to your own eating-management needs. You will find some more suitable than others. But you won't know which these are unless you try them!

Lifestyle changes produce gradual weight reduction, which research shows is more likely to result in *permanent* weight loss. This eliminates the "pendulum swing" of losing the same pounds over and over again! In this study, we will look at lifestyle change from God's perspective. As we seek to change habits and attitudes, the power of God's Word can lift us up, encourage us to have diligence and stamina, and give us a joy and reward far beyond that which purely human effort brings.

1

LEMON LAYER CAKE, ANYONE?

As she walked up the steps, Elizabeth resolved that she would not eat even one bite at the open house for some new neighbors on the street. At two o'clock in the afternoon she certainly wasn't hungry. As she walked in the door, she was greeted by friends and then immediately escorted by her hostess to a dining table laden with a delicious array of sweets. Someone placed a cup of punch in Elizabeth's hand while asking if she would prefer lemon layer cake or a pecan tart, then insisting that she try some of each. While she chatted with the other guests, Elizabeth was horrified to discover that she had devoured every morsel! She wondered what had happened to her good intentions. Although Elizabeth had firmly resolved not to eat anything at the party, she found herself a victim of social circumstances.

Human resolution without divine intervention will eventually fail. But we are not left to our own frail devices and determinations. In 2 Peter 1:4–6, Peter invites us to "participate in the divine nature" and then urges us on, saying, "For this very reason, make every effort to add to your faith goodness; and to goodness, knowledge; and to knowledge, *self-control*." By calling upon God's power we can gain self-control.

Most of us think of practicing self-control as drudgery, a discipline that can be downright stifling. We may say, "What could possibly be pleasant about not eating a piece of Boston cream pie?" Yet pleasing God with our obedience is absolutely liberating. We have a choice to make: living within the *bounds* of Christ or living in *bondage* to Boston cream pie. It is my prayer that God's Word will unlock the chains of your present eating lifestyle and point you to freedom through self-control.

Self-Discipline: A Fruit of the Spirit

1. Turn to Romans 7:15, 18–19. How do Paul's sentiments relate to your desire to lose weight and your present eating habits? ____________________

   ____

   ____

2. The conflict which Paul describes, as well as the conflict between weight reduction and overeating, shows lack of self-control. Yet God is the originator of order and discipline. As you read Genesis 1:1–19, note examples of God's orderliness. ____________________

   ____

   ____

3. How does God the Son exemplify self-discipline (Philippians 2:6–8)? ____________________

____

____

4. What is the last element of the fruit of the Spirit (Galatians 5:22–23)? __________ How does it complement the other elements of the fruit of the Spirit? ________

   ____

   ____

   a. Compare the terms "self-control" and "Spirit-control." ______________________________

   ____

   ____

   ____

   b. Write a definition of "Spirit-control": ____________

   ____

   ____

   ____

   c. Read Micah 3:8. What is your main resource for disciplined habits? _________________________

   ____

5. Read 2 Timothy 1:7. What do Paul's words mean in your new venture in weight reduction? ____________

   ____

6. The Lord promises to turn weakness into strength. He clearly says, "I will strengthen you and help you" (Isaiah 41:10). Yet to effectively call upon His strength, we must identify our danger areas. Turn to the Old Testament and read Nehemiah 4:7–9. What did Nehemiah and the

workers rebuilding the Jerusalem walls do when their enemies plotted against them? ____________________

____

____

7. Being constantly watchful for the enemy is necessary for protection. How does this apply to overeating in unplanned situations? ____________________

____

____

Responsibility and Commitment

1. Whom did Adam blame when explaining why he ate the fruit from the tree of knowledge of good and evil (Genesis 3:12)? ____________________

   Whom did Eve blame (Genesis 3:13)? ____________________

2. Although both Adam and Eve were tempted, who was ultimately responsible for their actions? ____________________

____

3. List any circumstances, relationships, or other factors that you blame for being overweight: ____________________

____

____

4. Although many of these factors may have directly influenced your weight, who is ultimately responsible?

____

5. Changing your eating pattern and attitude toward good requires time and perseverance. It requires a decision, a commitment to a new eating lifestyle. List several

attitudes or actions that you know reflect what your degree of commitment to weight reduction is: ________

____

____

____

____

6. Read Psalm 36:5. As you seek to be faithful in this new endeavor, consider God's faithfulness to you. How far does His faithfulness reach? ________________

7. What does God promise if we persevere (Galatians 6:9)?

____

To Do This Week

As you read in Nehemiah 4:7–9, setting a guard is an important response to danger. We too must be watchful to identify situations working against us while we are changing our eating patterns. This week, keep a record of every bite you eat . . . every cup of coffee . . . every lick of cake batter. You will find a sample food diary on page 26. Buy a spiral notebook to create your own, or photocopy the chart on page 28. Make a chart for each day.

Time Column: Record the time whenever you eat anything.

Place Column: When you ate were you in the kitchen, living room, bedroom, your office, a friend's house?

Associated Activity Column: While you were eating, were you watching television, washing dishes, playing bridge, driving, paying bills? (Bill-paying makes me overeat!)

Food and Amount Column: This column is very important. Give as much detail as possible. For instance:

- Don't just write "pork chops"; tell how many.
- Don't record "one helping mashed potatoes." Estimate. Was it half a cup? One cup?
- Don't write "a bunch of potato chips." Give an approximation (i.e., one handful, ten chips, or half of an eight-ounce bag).

This week you may tend to eat less to make the record look better. Try not to do this. This diary should reflect your *present* eating habits. No one will review this chart. It is for your benefit and analysis.

Pray together as a group for the discipline to faithfully complete each day's record.

Before beginning your week of record-keeping, write 2 Timothy 1:7 on a three-by-five card and tape it to your refrigerator door. Memorize it and be reminded that you can tap into the power of God to gain self-discipline.

Personal Reflection and Evaluation

Read Proverbs 22:3. Consider how Solomon's description of a prudent man applies to eating habits. Now examine your completed diary for any situations that led to unplanned or excess eating and answer the questions on page 29.

EXAMPLE:

TIME	PLACE	ASSOCIATED ACTIVITY	FOOD AND AMOUNT
8:00	kitchen	talking to children	½ c. Grape Nuts; ½ c. milk; 1 tsp. sugar
9:10	kitchen	washing dishes	Black coffee and English muffin; 1 tsp. margarine
12:00	patio	reading newspaper	ham and cheese sandwich (1 ounce each); apple; iced tea; 1 tsp. sugar

2 Timothy 1:7

For God did not give us a spirit of timidity, but a spirit of power, of love, and of self-discipline.

(NIV)

(To be completed during the week)

Date ________________

TIME	PLACE	ASSOCIATED ACTIVITY	FOOD AND AMOUNT

1. Was there anything unusual about this week (on vacation, house guests, holiday, party)? ______

______

2. Was there any particular time span during which you ate a lot (e.g., evening, midmorning)? ______

______

______

______

3. In what rooms of the house did you eat? ______

______

______

4. List any activities you did while eating (other than talking): ______

______

______

5. Were you surprised by anything you wrote down? ______

______

6. Name one helpful thing you learned about your eating habits. ______

______

Seek and Share

NOTE: In each chapter this section will contain activities for the group to complete after going over the preceding questions.

1. Divide into groups of three or four. List situations in each person's environment or pattern of daily living that may

be defeating her strongholds against overeating. Consider:

a. Time of day

b. Social situations

c. Meal preparation

d. Relaxation activities

e. Relationships

f. Emotions

2. As a group, commit yourselves to each other as together you begin to work toward self-control in weight reduction. Verbalize this commitment to the person sitting next to you. What is her name and address? ___________

____

3. This week, send her a note of encouragement, expressing your commitment to her.

2

SAVOR THE FRUIT

I love chocolate ice cream. It hits my taste buds and slides down my throat lickety split. Another spoonful quickly follows so that the taste will not be lost. What a cycle!

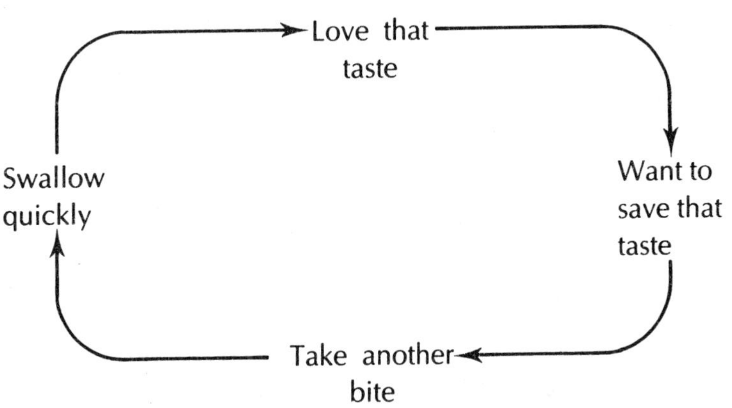

There I sit, with an empty dish and no satisfaction. My memory is blurred—"Did I really eat that?" And so, just for the taste, I eat another serving.

What I need to do is *take time to savor*. This will help me change my style of eating. It also has significant spiritual value as I seek to know God better. Let's explore both aspects of savoring—the practical and the spiritual.

To Savor . . . To Delight In

1. Read 1 Samuel 14:24–30. What was Jonathan's reaction to tasting honey? ______________________

2. Read Song of Songs 2:3. How does Beloved describe her lover? ______________________

   ____

3. Turn to Song of Songs 5:1. How does the lover describe his bride? ______________________

   ____

4. Write a definition of "savor." ______________________

   ____

   ____

5. As you read the following passages, consider how you can "savor the Lord."

   Psalm 119:103 ______________________

   ____

   Psalm 19:9–10 ______________________

   ____

   Hebrews 6:4–5 ______________________

   ____

1 Peter 2:2–3 ________________________________

____

6. Read Psalm 34:8. List ways to "taste and see" (experience) the presence of God. ____________________

   ____

   Recall one experience where you delighted in—savored—His presence.

   ____

   ____

   ____

   ____

   ____

   ____

Whoa! Savoring Takes Time

1. Note when you begin and end your next meal. (Use a typical situation, not a long lunch with a friend. Count only *eating* time.) How long did it take? ________ minutes.

2. Did you eat at approximately the same pace throughout your meal? ______________________________

3. Did you pause completely at any time? ____________

4. Relate Proverbs 19:2 to eating style. ______________

   ____

Too Fast, Too Full

1. When was the last time you got up from the table, feeling too full, wondering why you had a second helping? ______

   ____

2. Eating without pausing is usually the cause of that frustrating "too full" feeling. Your fork is quicker than your nervous system's feedback system. This is what happens when you eat:

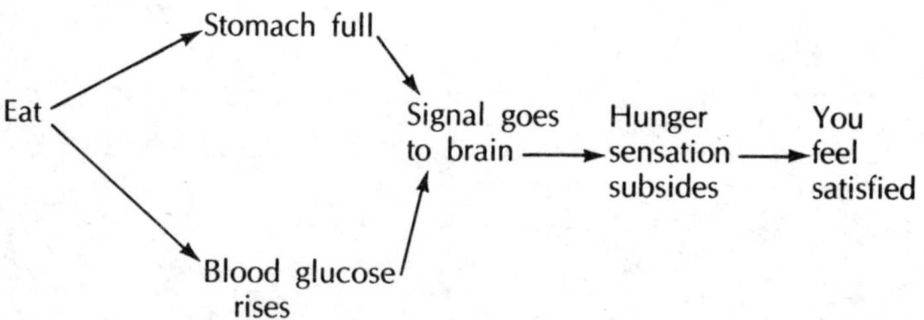

   When you eat fast, without pausing, you do not allow time for your brain to get the "full signal." This results in overeating and an overstuffed feeling later on.

3. Read Proverbs 25:16. How much does Solomon tell us to eat? ______________________________

4. The following strategies for slowing your eating will help you follow Solomon's advice.

   a. Swallow your mouthful before adding more to your fork. What are you usually doing while you chew and swallow? ______________________________

   b. Put your fork down on your plate between bites. This may seem awkward at first, but it will gradually break the habit of constant motion while you eat.

Analyze your habits. For one minute during your meal, count the number of times you put your fork down. This will be your eating ratio.

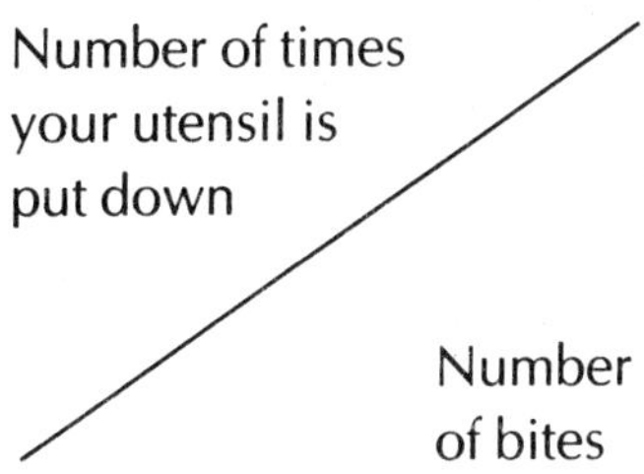

For example, if you took ten bites and laid your fork down once, your ratio is 1/10. Your goal is to eat at a 1/1 ratio.

c. Create a method to remind yourself to savor your food. This could be a three-by-five card with "Fork Down" in red letters, or a pretty silk flower at your place setting. It can be practical or silly. No one else even needs to know about it. What will be your cue? ______

____

d. Once you have reached a 1/1 ratio, then stop eating for two minutes. Relax, talk, carry on as usual, then resume eating.

e. Enjoy your food. You need not feel guilty about eating if you choose to eat in the proper place with the proper method. Reveling in the taste helps prevent "closet eating"—eating quickly and secretly so no one will know.

To Do This Week

Record your eating ratio and minutes spent eating at each meal or snack. This is like practicing the piano—it's tedious, but you'll be glad you did it.

	Example	Day 1	Day 2	Day 3	Day 4	Day 5	Day 6	Day 7
Breakfast	1/10 5 min.							
Lunch	1/8 12 min.							
Dinner	1/8 15 min.							
Snacks	1/10 2 min.							
	1/5 3 min.							

This week savor your food, and spend time also savoring the goodness of our Lord. Meditate on God's goodness to the Israelites and on God's goodness to you!

"They captured fortified cities and fertile land; they took possession of houses filled with all kinds of good things, wells already dug, vineyards, olive groves and fruit trees in abundance. *They ate to the full and were well-nourished; they reveled in your [God's] great goodness*" (Nehemiah 9:25, italics mine).

Seek and Share

1. The leader of your group should ask someone to bring a food item for taste-testing to the meeting. It can even be

sweet, like pumpkin bread or cookies. Choose an item that has hard-to-identify ingredients such as spices. After each person has a portion, pass out paper and pencils, and do the following exercise:

a. Look at the food item. Write down *exactly* what you see. Use descriptive words (i.e., the cookie is light brown, crumbly, and has little dark flecks). ____________

____

____

b. Smell it. Describe what you experience (i.e., the muffin smells like cinnamon and apples). ____________

____

____

c. Take a bite, concentrating on the texture. What do you feel? ______________________________________

____

d. Take another bite, concentrating on the taste. Let it sit in your mouth for a few seconds. Describe exactly what you taste. ______________________________

____

____

2. Partnership in Weight Reduction.

a. Read 1 Samuel 23:15–17.

What did Jonathan do for David (verse 16)? ____________

____

____

How does Jonathan assure David? ____________________

____

How can you apply this example of friendship to another person in your group? ____________________

____

____

b. Turn to Hebrews 3:13. How can you apply this concept to weight reduction? ____________________

____

c. Now read Deuteronomy 3:28. What does the Lord tell Moses to do for Joshua, who is to lead the Israelites? ____

____

d. Read Judges 20:22a. What did the men of Israel do?

____

____

e. Separate with the person you sent a note of encouragement to last week. Together, ask the Lord for a motivated spirit to change habits and for enthusiasm in this new endeavor.

3

GREEN LIGHTS ... CAUTION ... STOP

Imagine . . .

It's 8:45. You are on your way to an appointment downtown. For breakfast you had shredded wheat with sugar and milk, orange juice, and black coffee. As you make your way down the street you notice business people walking briskly. You pass an elderly woman waiting for the bus. You are aware of many people on their way to various activities and responsibilities. A bus is pulling up to the bus stop. You hear the screech of the brakes, you smell the exhaust—that musty, fumy smell.

A sweet fragrance fights its way through the exhaust to your nose. It becomes stronger. You finally identify the smell of freshly baked bread, cinnamon, brown sugar. It becomes intense as you walk by the bakery. In the one-second glance through the window you see turnovers—blueberry, apple, and cherry; sticky buns—plain or with raisins and nuts;

pumpkin, lemon, and molasses pies; cinnamon bread; gingerbread cookies; bread in every shape and size; lemon and prune breakfast rings; blueberry, cherry, and apple tarts; doughnuts—sugar-coated, chocolate-iced, cream-filled, French! Are you hungry? What do you do?

—Do you walk on by?
—Do you consider going in?
—Do you go in and buy a tart?

What made you hungry? Sight and smell can be green lights creating an uncontrollable, unplanned urge to eat. It happens when you notice a candy dish or when you eye Twinkies on top of the refrigerator. It happens when you walk by a vending machine or when you stop at McDonald's for a Coke and then smell the French fries. Much television advertising is based on this concept. Who doesn't drool over a close-up of butter melting on syrup-laden pancakes? It looks real; it almost smells—you want some, right now.

Just as an actor listens for the cue which prompts his next line, we find cues that prompt us to eat. They are "eating cues," saying "Eat." "Eat me now."

When eating is repeatedly coupled with another activity or a particular place, we eventually feel hungry whenever we do that activity or go to that place. This occurs despite the absence of physiological need. These cues include watching television, reading or studying, driving, and celebrating an event. Becoming aware of these cues in our daily living is the first step in suppressing them.

Fix Your Gaze Directly Before You (Proverbs 4:25)

1. What was the cue that initiated David's adulterous invitation to Bathsheba (2 Samuel 11:2–3)?

   ____

2. What compelled Samson to spend the night with a prostitute (Judges 16:1)? ______________________________

3. How do the temptations of David and Samson relate to eating cues? ______________________________________

   ____

4. What is tempting you by sight? Take time right now to walk through your home. Do you see candy on the coffee table, cookies in a glass jar, or bananas on top of the refrigerator? Store everything out of sight, either in cupboards or in opaque containers. List the items you have removed or rearranged.

   ____________________ ____________________

   ____________________ ____________________

   ____________________ ____________________

   ____________________ ____________________

   ____________________ ____________________

   ____________________ ____________________

5. What will God provide in our temptation (1 Corinthians 10:13)? ______________________________________

   ____

6. Serving dishes on the table are another cue. Removing them from the table after everyone is served or serving each plate beforehand may help you avoid unwanted second helpings.

The Tick of the Clock

1. Try to place yourself in the following circumstance:

   It is 12:00 noon and you are manning a crafts booth at the community bazaar. Your replacement is due at 12:30. There are fixings for a ham and cheese sandwich and fruit for lunch in your refrigerator at home. The booth next to yours is selling baked goods. Do you:

   a. *not* think about food, just assuming you will have lunch at home? ____________________

   b. purposefully avoid buying a sweet knowing it will spoil your lunch? ____________________

   c. buy a couple of cookies to tide you over until you can eat lunch around 1? ____________________

   d. enjoy some baked items and forget eating lunch at all?

   Studies show that if you are overweight, you will probably choose choices "c" or "d."

2. What does this tell you about time and eating cues?

   ____

   ____

   ____

3. The same time or event can be interpreted differently and result in different food choices. This is true spiritually also. Read 1 Corinthians 1:18 and catch a glimpse of the importance of perception. Notes: ____________________

   ____

   ____

4. Review your diary from the first week. Reflect on this past week too.

a. Other than regular meal times, is there a specific time of day at which you repeatedly eat without meaning to? ______________________________

____

____

b. Do you ever eat before a meal to tide you over? ______

____

____

____

Where Are You?

1. Read Jonah 1:1–17. Where was Jonah supposed to go?

   ____

2. Where did he go instead? ______________________________

   ____

3. What happened to Jonah because he was in the wrong place? ______________________________

   ____

   ____

4. Jonah was disobedient to God by going toward Tarshish instead of Nineveh. He was in the wrong place, and he paid for it. There are consequences to being in the wrong place. How does this apply to eating habits? __________

   ____

5. Look back at your first week's diary. List the rooms/places in which you ate (i.e., kitchen, den, car).

   ______________ ______________

____________________ ____________________

____________________ ____________________

____________________ ____________________

____________________ ____________________

____________________ ____________________

6. As you look at the diary, reflect on a time when you ate somewhere other than in the kitchen or dining room or at a restaurant (for instance, in the den or bedroom). How aware were you of what and *how much* you were eating? Circle one:

   (totally unaware) 1 2 3 4 5 6 7 8 9 10 (very aware)

7. Read Jeremiah 50:24a. In what state of awareness was Babylon caught? ____________________

   ____

   Eating in inappropriate places decreases your awareness of the amount you eat and sets a trap for overeating.

8. This week work at eating in designated places. For instance:

   Breakfast should be eaten at the kitchen table.

   —Don't drink your orange juice in the bedroom.

   —Don't eat your cereal at the counter as you prepare bag lunches.

   Lunch and *dinner* should be eaten at the table or in a restaurant.

   —Avoid eating in front of the TV. (Some people who live alone enjoy eating while watching TV. If this does not create a problem in controlling your eating, go ahead.)

Snacks should be eaten at the kitchen or dining room table, *with* a place setting. This is probably the most important food to eat in a designated area.

What Are You Doing?

1. Read Luke 10:38–42. How is Martha distracted from listening to Jesus? ____________________

2. Imagine Martha working in the kitchen area and trying to hear what Jesus had to say too. How well could she concentrate on Jesus? ____________________

3. What usually happens when you try to concentrate on two things at once? ____________________

   ____

4. What happens when you eat and do another activity such as reading or watching TV at the same time? ________

   ____

5. Look back at your first week's diary and list the activities you did (other than talking) while eating.

   ____________ ____________

   ____________ ____________

   ____________ ____________

   ____________ ____________

   ____________ ____________

   ____________ ____________

6. Think of a specific time when you ate and did something else at the same time.

a. How aware were you of how much you ate?

Circle one:

(totally unaware) 1 2 3 4 5 6 7 8 9 10 (very aware)

b. Had you planned to eat? ____________________

c. Did you eat more than you had planned? __________

When we are doing two things at once (such as eating and reading), one activity is at the forefront of our thinking, while the other is more unconscious. Eating usually becomes *unconscious.* We are *unaware* of what we are doing and usually fall into the trap of overeating.

7. Go back to Luke 10:38–42. What was Mary doing? ____

____

What was her level of concentration as she listened to Jesus?

____

8. Read over the New Habit Strategy on the next page.

To Do This Week

1. This week keep track of all food eaten between meals. Make seven copies of the chart on page 48. In the right-hand column, record any cues which influenced your eating. For example:

—The banana was on the table
—It was noon
—My husband was snacking
—I walked by the vending machine
—Doughnuts were present at the staff meeting

New Habit Strategy for the Week

Avoid extra, unaccounted-for, unplanned calories.

—Avoid eating while preparing meals.
a slice of ham while making a sandwich
a smidgen of grated cheese that belongs in a casserole
crackers while preparing dinner

—Avoid eating while driving.
breakfast on the way to work
a bag of cheese puffs
a Coke

—Avoid eating while reading.
reading the newspaper at the breakfast table
snacking while studying or working

—Avoid eating while watching television.

—Remember, if you want a snack, set a place setting at the table.

2. Be in contact midweek with the person you prayed with in last week's meeting. Share any changes you have made in your eating style. Release some frustration if you wish, but do not dwell on it. Call each other when you need encouragement.

   Hebrews 3:13: "Encourage one another daily."

Date ________________

TIME	PLACE	ASSOCIATED ACTIVITY	FOOD AND AMOUNT	EATING CUE

Seek and Share

1. Reflect on the past week and describe any instances when you consciously chose not to eat while doing another activity. ______________________

____

____

2. How did eating snacks in a designated area affect frequency of snacking, the amount you ate, and your attitude toward the snack? ______________________

____

____

3. Were you more aware of what you ate this week? ______

____

4. Review this week's diary. What three cues most often led you to eat? ______________________

____

____

5. Compare the "Associated Activity" columns of week one and of this week's diaries. ______________________

____

____

6. Compare the "Place" column of week one and of this week's diaries. ______________________

____

7. What does God say about persevering against temptation (James 1:12)? ______________________

____

4

FOOTSTEPS TO FOLLOW

In our struggle to change our lifestyle, our human capabilities often fall far short of our goals. Self-discipline however, when sought within the context of God's resources, is attainable. Jesus had a disciplined yet casual lifestyle. As the God-man, He was perfect—and He was given to us as a model.

We are called to "be imitators of God" (Ephesians 5:1). God has graciously provided Christ , the perfect model and the Holy Spirit, the perfect facilitator. First Peter 2:21 says, "To this you were called, because Christ suffered for you, *leaving you an example,* that you should follow in his footsteps." Come see how far His footsteps go. *

*Much of the material in this chapter has been adapted from *Control Yourself: Practicing the Art of Self-Discipline* by G. G. Kehl, published by Zondervan, 1982.

Glory Came Down

1. Consider how discipline was evidenced by God the Father (John 3:16). ______
2. Describe how Christ's coming required discipline (Philippians 2:6–7). ______
3. How does Jesus demonstrate self-control in His boyhood (Luke 2:51)? ______

Temptation in the Desert

Read Matthew 4:1–11.

1. What was Jesus' first act of discipline in the desert (v. 2)?
   ______
2. List three ways Satan tempted Jesus. ______
   ______
   ______
3. On what basis did Jesus refuse Satan and show self-control? ______
4. What state was Jesus in when Satan tempted Him to turn stones into bread (vv. 1–3)? ______
   ______

   What does this tell you about Satan's strategy for gaining control? ______
   ______
5. Why were these temptations all worth the struggle (Hebrews 2:18)? ______

Balance—An Evidence of Discipline

1. Read John 11:32–40. Describe the balance between Christ's sorrow (vv. 33–35) and His joy (v. 40). ______

____

____

____

2. Read Luke 19:41–46. Describe Christ's balance between feeling (v. 41) and action (v. 45). ____________

____

____

____

3. Read John 2:13–16. What is the basis for Jesus' anger? In what way is His anger disciplined? ______________

____

____

____

Preparing for Death

1. How does Jesus set out for Jerusalem (Luke 9:51)? ______

____

2. a. What emotions did Jesus feel before His death (Mark 14:32–36)? ______________________________

   b. How does He evidence discipline in His prayer to the Father? ______________________________

3. How does Christ evidence self-discipline in His statement to the disciples (John 10:17–18)? ______________

____

4. How does Christ handle His divine power in obedience to God's will (Matthew 26:53–54)? ______________

____

5. What is Jesus' reply to the chief priests and elders and to Pontius Pilate (Matthew 27:12–14)? ____________________

   ____

6. List ways Christ manifested self-discipline (Isaiah 50:4–7). ____

   ____

   ____

7. What is Christ's final disciplined act (John 19:30)? ________

   ____

8. Write a summary paragraph on Christ's self-discipline.

   ____

   ____

   ____

   ____

   ____

   ____

   ____

   ____

To Do This Week

1. Every time you are tempted to eat at an inappropriate time or place, or an inappropriate amount, step back for just a moment. Reflect on just *one* way Christ demonstrated self-discipline. Consider its impact on you. Ask the Lord to give you the strength to discipline your eating habits. Praise and thank Him when you are successful.

Remember, failure does not mean we are less spiritual. It's just a reminder that we are mere mortals, striding along as best we can in Jesus' footsteps.

2. Call your prayer partner. Encourage her with Titus 2:11–13: "For the grace of God that brings salvation has appeared to all men. It teaches us to say 'No' to ungodliness and worldly passions, and to live self-controlled, upright and godly lives in this present age."
3. As, with Christ's help, you consciously refuse the urge to eat, record on page 55 the thought that helped you discipline yourself.

Seek and Share

1. When you felt tempted to eat, which instance of Christ's self-discipline did you most often reflect on? ______________

   ____

   Was it helpful in your decision? ______________________
   Name one food item you refused because of Christ's example. ______________________________________
2. How does the self-discipline of Christ almost two thousand years ago affect us today? __________________

   ____

   ____

   ____
3. Share and reflect on the following verses as you consider Christ's enabling power through the Holy Spirit.

   Micah 3:8a ______________________________________

   ____

   ____

Date	Specific episode, characteristic, or thought about Christ that gave you self-control.

Ephesians 3:16 ______________________________

____

____

Romans 8:9 ______________________________

____

____

Conclude in prayer, remembering Hebrews 1:3: "The Son is the radiance of God's glory and the exact representation of his being." Pray for the power to walk in His footsteps.

5

UNLOCKING THE CHAINS

What did you do before sitting down to do your Bible study? ________. And before that? ________. And before that? ________. Everything we do is a link in a series of events, or a behavior chain. It has a beginning and an ending. And it can be positive or negative. Here is an example of a homemaker's habitual negative eating chain.

An inappropriate eating chain can occur very quickly, with little forewarning. As in this example, links in the chain can appear quite harmless, yet continually end in unplanned, guilt-producing eating. Let's find the key to unlock negative chains of overeating.

How to Break a Chain

1. Look at the example of the homemaker on page 58. At what point did she head in the direction of eating? Draw a line where this occurred.

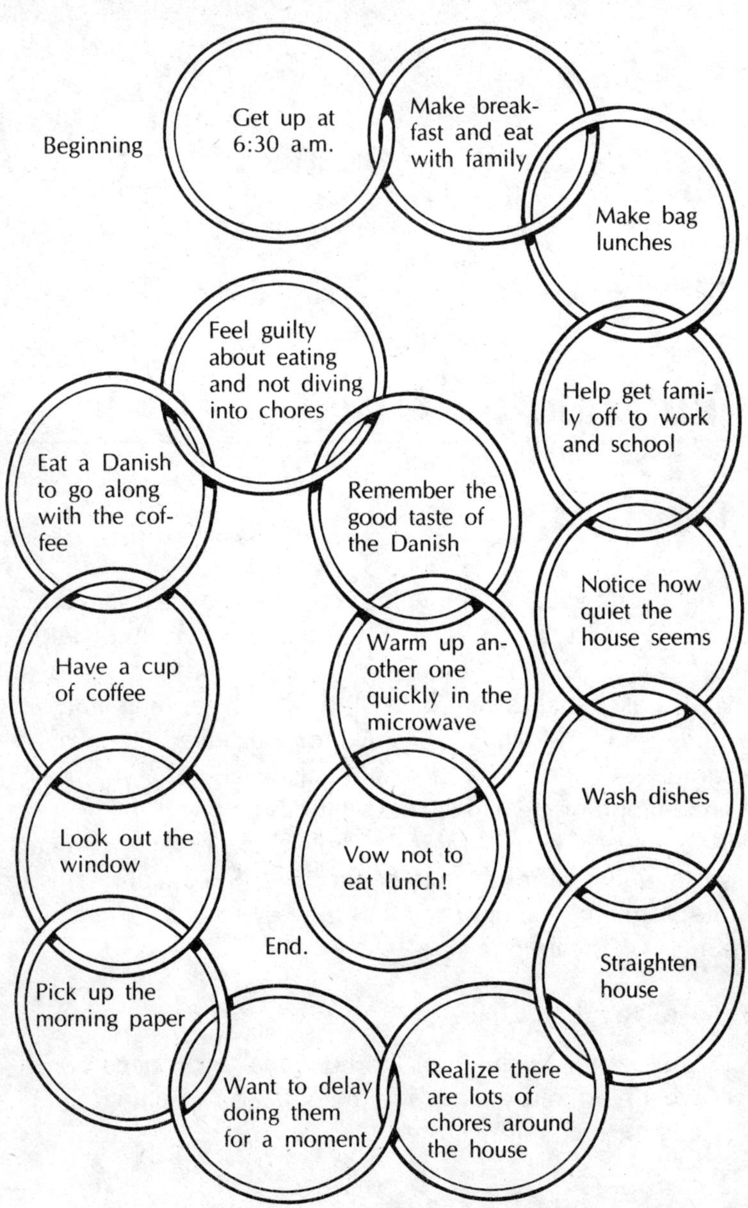
Beginning
Get up at 6:30 a.m.
Make break-fast and eat with family
Make bag lunches
Help get fami-ly off to work and school
Notice how quiet the house seems
Wash dishes
Straighten house
Realize there are lots of chores around the house
Want to delay doing them for a moment
Pick up the morning paper
Look out the window
Have a cup of coffee
Eat a Danish to go along with the cof-fee
Feel guilty about eating and not diving into chores
Remember the good taste of the Danish
Warm up an-other one quickly in the microwave
Vow not to eat lunch!
End.

2. Where should she have tried to break the chain?________

____

3. Breaking a behavior chain is like correcting a travel mistake.

If you want to go to Greenwood, but missed Exit 1, and you do not want to go into New York City, what do you do? ____________________________________

____

4. Just as you would *take* an alternate route, you must *do* an alternate activity to initiate a new chain of events. List activities you can and are willing to do to break a chain. They must compete with the urge to eat and be easily available to do.

   Example:

Pleasant Activities	*Necessary Activities*
call Mary Jane	clean the refrigerator
________________	________________
________________	________________
________________	________________
________________	________________

____________________ ____________________

____________________ ____________________

Copy these activities onto a three-by-five card and tape it to the refrigerator door. (No one needs to know why; they can just assume you are organized!) When you realize you are in a chain directed toward inappropriate eating, go to your list. Determine to do one activity, with the understanding that if you still greatly desire to eat afterward, you may. In most cases, however, your desire will be gone. You have started a *new* behavior chain and taken an alternate route.

Why does this work? The desire to eat (which can be manifested by actual hunger pangs without physiological need) lasts only ten or fifteen minutes. You have endured this dangerous time and diverted your mind to another activity.

If you still decide to eat, it is *not* failure. You have thought about it and *chosen* to eat, rather than eating in an unplanned style. Remember to eat in an appropriate place in the absence of competing activity, and savor your food *slowly*.

5. Sometimes you do not identify a chain until you are at the last link, standing in front of the refrigerator. If so, set the kitchen timer for ten or fifteen minutes and run to the other side of the house and *do* something. (Clean out a drawer!) You may be pleasantly surprised, when the timer dings, that you have totally forgotten why!

A Negative Chain Unbroken

Read 1 Samuel 18. Then fill in the chain of events leading to Saul's being David's lifelong enemy.

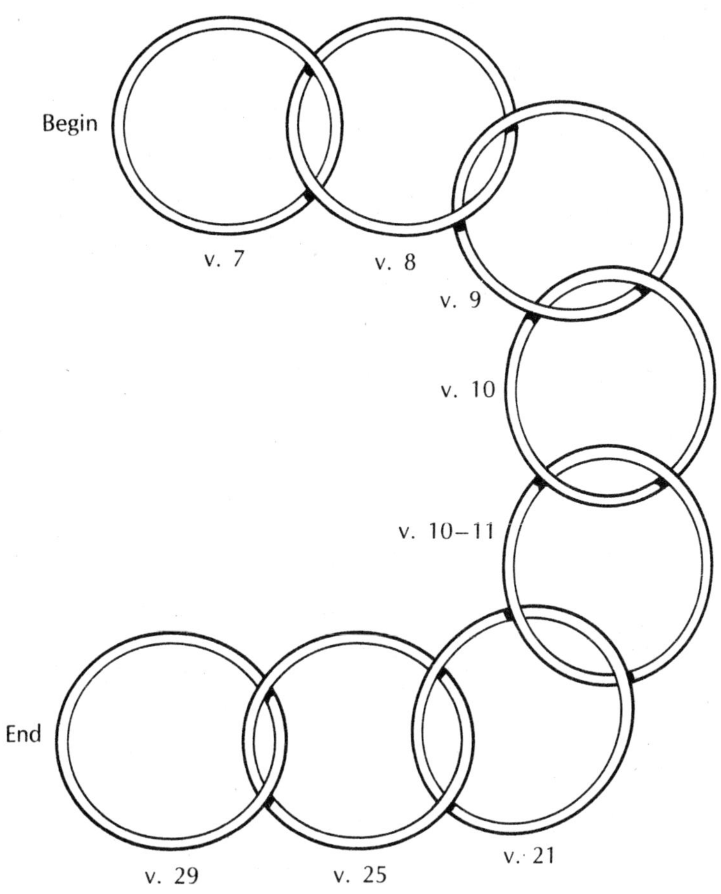

God Seeks Us Out

1. Fill in Saul's (Paul's) behavior chain on page 62 as you read the verses.

2. How was Paul's chain of hateful acts toward the early Christians changed? ______________________________

____

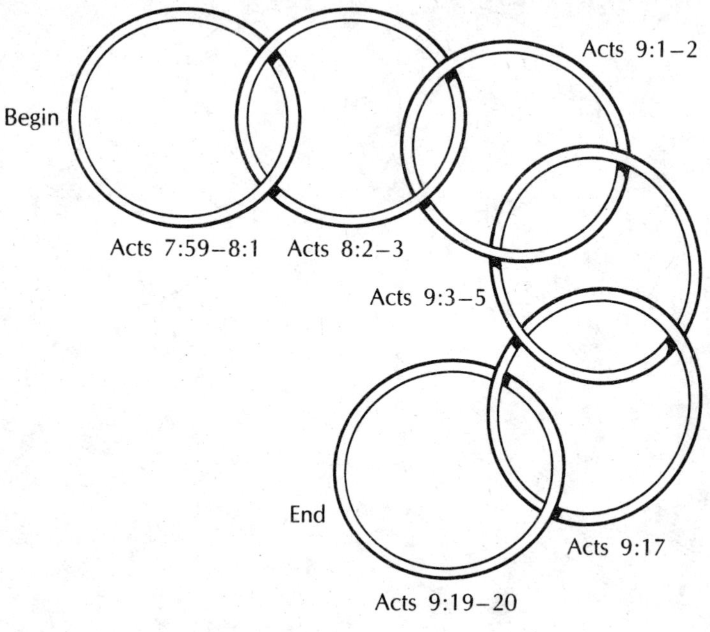

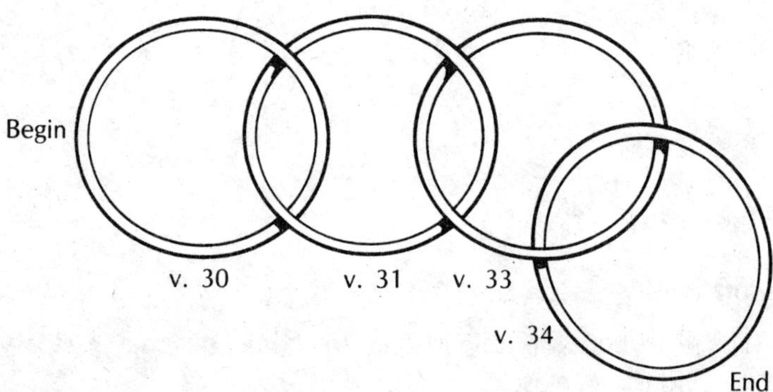

We Seek God Out

1. Read Daniel 4. Fill in the chain of events as King Nebuchadnezzar's dream was fulfilled.

2. How was Nebuchadnezzar's chain of events broken?

____

____

3. How does this relate to our breaking a negative eating chain? ____

____

4. What is the chain of events in uncontrolled temptation (James 1:13–15)? ____

____

____

5. What is our protection against temptation?

   Psalm 119:11 ____

   Luke 22:46 ____

6. Read Genesis 39:7–12. What did Joseph do when tempted by Potiphar's wife? ____

____

To Do This Week

1. Keep a log of each chain that you break. (See page 64.)
2. Fill in a negative eating chain you observed this week. You may have to work backward from the actual eating episode. (See page 65.)

Seek and Share

1. How does the power of God help us break negative eating chains? ____

Date	Time	Alternate Activity

____

____

2. List other biblical characters who broke a negative chain by seeking out God or by God's direct intervention. ____

____

3. Separate from the group with your prayer partner. Share and pray together as you read 2 Samuel 22:2.

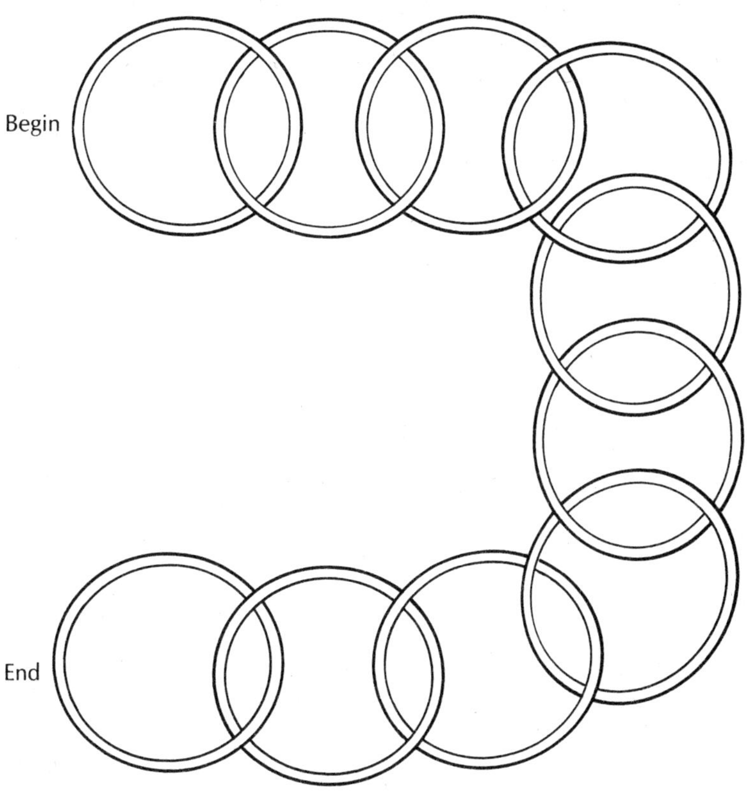
Begin
End

6

GOD'S FOOD, GOD'S BODY

Many of us have difficulty placing the care of our bodies high on our scale of priorities. As Christians, we do not want to be preoccupied by appearance. We cringe at today's overemphasis on "body beautiful" techniques and apparel. Yet in our desire to "seek first his kingdom and his righteousness" (Matthew 6:33), we may make the mistake of ignoring our bodies.

In our quest for physical self-discipline, we will be confused about how to treat our bodies if we have a distorted view of their role. Do we ignore them, deplore them, or adore them? Or do we view them as "fearfully and wonderfully made" (Psalm 139:14)?

A House of Jewels

1. Why does your body deserve good care (Genesis 1:27)?

____

2. What gives dignity to our human form?

   John 1:14 ____________________

   Philippians 2:7–8 ____________________

3. What is your body? What does it hold (1 Corinthians 3:16)?

   ____

   a. 2 Corinthians 4:6–7. What does Paul mean by "treasure"? ____________________
   and "jars of clay"? ____________________

   b. 2 Corinthians 4:10. What do we carry around in our bodies? ____________________
   What is revealed in our bodies? ____________________

   ____

4. What does God ask us to do with our bodies (2 Corinthians 7:1)? ____________________

   ____

   How does this apply to what and how much we eat? ____

   ____

   ____

   ____

5. How should we regard our bodies? What is our responsibility toward our bodies? ____________________

   ____

   ____

   ____

6. How does Scripture describe our bodies as we offer them up to God (Romans 12:1)? ______________________

____

7. How should the creation and role of our bodies affect our care for our physical selves? ______________________

____

____

Confidence in the One Who Supplies

1. Although we pay for our food with money at the grocery store, who is the ultimate provider?

   Psalm 111:5 ______________________________

   Psalm 136:25 _____________________________

   Psalm 145:15 _____________________________

2. Even when the Israelites were in the desert,

   a. How did God feed them (Exodus 16:14–16)? ________

   b. What was the bread called? What did it look and taste like (Exodus 16:31)? ______________________

   ____

   c. How long did the Israelites eat manna (Exodus 16:35)?

   ____

   d. Read Exodus 16:4. How does this apply to our eating habits? ______________________________

   ____

3. Recognizing God's provision, how should we make good use of our food? ______________________

____

When my two-year-old has eaten enough cheese and apple slices, that's it! She presses her lips together with a determined grimace as if to say, "You can't make me eat it." She is well aware when her stomach is full and her needs are met. Then I think, "That piece of cheese on her plate is hardly worth the effort to wrap and refrigerate, and I certainly can't throw it away, so I guess I'll eat it." Sound familiar?

Many of us grew up finishing our plates on behalf of "the starving children in India." And today, in the name of good stewardship, we continue to eat the last bite. Somehow we feel that if it's in our stomach, it is put to good use! So what do you do with the extra five peas at the bottom of the bowl, the last serving of mashed potatoes, or that one lonely slice of meat? I challenge you, as a conscientious Christian, to find creative alternatives to eating the last bite.

To Do This Week

Record on the chart on page 70 each time you use leftovers creatively or throw out unusable food. You might enjoy contributing fifty cents to a group project (see next section) each time you throw unusable food away.

Seek and Share

1. Making good use of our resources includes using leftovers properly. This also helps combat the eating-the-last-bite syndrome. Leftovers need to be assigned a duty however, or else they end up in our mouths or covered with mold in the recesses of the refrigerator.

   a. As a group, list ways to use leftovers *right away*. (For example: making up tomorrow's sandwich with leftover meat before you do the dishes.)

   ____

Date	Food used as leftover	Food thrown out

____

____

____

b. Make a commitment to try one of the leftovers suggestions. Write it on a three-by-five card and put it above the kitchen sink. What do you choose to do?

____

2. Some leftovers are difficult to use. What do you do with two bites of a grilled cheese sandwich? If you have to choose between your stomach and the garbage, throw it in the garbage! Eating it cannot help the needy.

3. Come to Bible study this week prepared to contribute to a fund for those in need. Choose as a group one of the following:

   a. If you are aware of a needy family in your church or community, send them an anonymous gift certificate to a local grocery store.

   b. Send a contribution to an organization that can help others in need. Some suggestions are:

      World Relief
      P.O. Box WRC
      Wheaton, IL 60187

      World Vision International
      919 West Huntington Drive
      Monrovia, CA 91016

      Compassion International
      P.O. Box 7000
      3955 Cragwood Drive
      Colorado Springs, CO 80933

   c. Contribute to your local food bank for those in need.

   d. Buy dried and canned foods for a food closet in your church, established for those in need within your fellowship. If your church has no food closet, organize one.

What did you as a group decide on? ____________________

____

Choose someone to carry on to completion with the help of others in the group: ____________________

7

MADE IN THE IMAGE OF GOD

Whenever we open a magazine or turn on the television, we are bombarded with consumer messages.

> "Lorean Condition brings back the bounce in your hair." (Have you ever seen a homely girl on a commercial?)
>
> "Use Quans Cream for healthier, younger-looking skin."
>
> "Phillips Jeans fit just right." (On a perfect derriere.)
>
> "Your prince will knock at your door when you drink Carlisle White Wine."

Even as we consciously respond, "Oh, how silly!" we are poked, prodded, pinched, and ultimately influenced. We start questioning ourselves if we don't fit society's image. Looking just right is a driving goal today. According to advertisers, your physical appearance tells us who you are, what you do, and what you value. We so easily get pulled in by the undertow of all these messages. Directly or indirectly, they influence our self-image and feeling of self-worth.

Society's image leaves no place for overweight women. Let's face it: everything from clothes to cars is made for skinny people. We are told a woman should be super slim. She should have the sleek model image. This is indeed an unreal expectation for most women, and in some cases it can prove very unhealthy. But whether we believe them or not, society's messages influence our self-image.

—Define "self-image" (use a dictionary if you wish). ______

____

____

—Who or what influences your self-image? ____________

____

____

—Write descriptive words or phrases which reflect your personal opinion of yourself. ______________________

____

____

—How can your self-image differ from who you really are? ______________________________________

____

____

—How do the reactions of others regarding your weight affect your self-image? ___________________________

Custom-Made by God

As Christians, we cannot allow our self-image to depend on the outside world. Our self-worth comes from God—let's remind ourselves of that. I invite you to look into God's Word and find the true significance of your personal worth.

1. Read Psalm 139:14–15 and reflect on your creation.

   a. How were you designed? ______________________________

   ____

   b. What does this tell you about every feature you possess? ______________________________

   ____

   c. God custom-made you; how does He regard your value? ______________________________

   ____

2. How is God's love for you measured?

   a. Jeremiah 31:3 ______________________________

   b. Romans 8:38–39 ______________________________

   ____

   c. Ephesians 3:17–19 ______________________________

   ____

   d. Take a few moments and reflect upon these descriptions. Bask in His love. How does God's love affect your self-image? ______________________________

   ____

Christ Knows You and Loves You

As you complete the following questions, reflect on how personal God is.

1. How well does God know us (Matthew 10:30)? ________

____

2. In knowing us so well, what does God say about us?

   Isaiah 53:6 ____________________________

   1 John 1:8 ____________________________

   Romans 3:23 ___________________________

   What is the consequence of sin (Romans 6:23)?

   ____

3. Write an off-the-cuff definition of "sin." __________

   ____

   ____

4. What is the alternative to the consequence of sin? Who provides it?

   1 John 2:1–2 __________________________

   John 3:16 _____________________________

5. Read 1 Peter 3:18. From this passage explain Christ's role. ________________________________

   ____

   ____

   ____

6. Reflect on 1 John 5:11–13. Briefly explain how you can be assured of eternal life. ________________

   ____

   ____

   ____

God Trusts You

As you read the following Scripture, reflect on all God entrusts to you.

1. What privilege does God give us? What does He reveal to us (John 15:15)? ______

______

2. What responsibility does God entrust to us (2 Corinthians 5:18–20)? ______

______

3. How does being a part of the body of believers in Christ "increase your value" (1 Corinthians 12:14–20)? ______

______

______

4. What are we called?

   1 John 3:1 ______

   Romans 8:17 ______

Personal Reflection and Action

1. How can setting too high goals affect your self-image? ______

______

2. Take a few moments and reflect. Are your goals for weight reduction small and challenging? Or are they too high, decreasing your opportunity for achievement?

______

______

3. How can setting appropriate goals affect your opinion of yourself? ______________________________

   ____

4. What is your major measurement stick for achievement in weight reduction—the scale, or changed eating behavior? ______________________________

5. List changes you have made in your eating style since you began this study. Flip back to past chapters as a reminder. ______________________________

   ____

   ____

   ____

6. Has your opinion of yourself changed since you began this study? If so, how? ________________________

   ____

7. Evaluating ourselves involves constructive criticism, but it also means giving credit where credit is due. Choose two or three changes you listed above.

   Regularly remind yourself of these accomplishments. Choose a reminder cue, such as every red light or every time you put a load of laundry in.

8. Ask loved ones to withhold criticism and affirm your achievements. Discuss your feelings and goals with someone who is close to you. Who are you going to ask for reinforcement? ________________________

   Do not hesitate to remind others when you especially need reinforcement.

9. Write a new definition of who you are today. ________

____

____

10. We cannot deny the weaknesses in our lives, but we can recognize what God does with them. What will He do in our weakness (2 Corinthians 12:9)? ____________

____

11. Take a moment to dedicate your weaknesses to God. Give them up to Him, asking Him to turn those weaknesses into Christ's power to create a positive change in your eating lifestyle.

To Do This Week

1. Encourage your prayer partner's self-image by writing a note appreciating a lovely, godly characteristic she possesses. Put it in the mail today, so she receives it before you meet again.
2. This week, keep a detailed food diary in your notebook, using the same type of chart as in chapter three. Have it filled out and ready for next week's lesson.

Seek and Share

1. Read 1 Peter 1:18–19. Discuss how the worth of the "object" that paid for your life reflects upon your personal worth.
2. Discuss the special needs an overweight individual has for an improved self-image (e.g., body image, social situations, family interactions). Pray as a group for insight and healing.

8

REST THE HORSES

My husband's grandfather, now ninety-six years old and a great man of God, gave this response when asked to give advice to our generation: "Take time to rest the horses."

We have thundered through this study, exploring new concepts and trying to apply them to our personal lifestyle. It's time to see how far we've gone and to determine where we desire to go from here. Let's "take time to rest the horses."

1. Prepare your heart for self-examination as you reflect on the following verses:

   Notes

   Psalm 26:2 ______________________________

   Psalm 119:59 ______________________________

   Lamentations 3:40 ______________________________

Haggai 1:7 ______________________________

2. Consider how your attitude and commitment have changed since you began this course.

   a. Turn back to page 24, question 5. As you review the question and your answer, consider the following:

   —Has your attitude about weight reduction changed since you began this study? If so, how? __________

   ____

   ____

   —What is your present degree of commitment to weight reduction? ______________________________

   b. What does David tell us to do (Psalm 37:5)? ________

   ____

   c. What does God promise us if we commit our endeavor to Him (Psalm 37:6)? ______________________________

   ____

3. Consider how cue elimination is providing you with safeguards against unplanned eating.

   a. Stroll through your kitchen. Is all food out of sight? ____

   b. Look back to your food log from week one and compare with last week's diary.

   —Have you made any changes in the time of day that you eat? Explain. ______________________________

   ____

   —What is your present attitude toward time and the need to eat? For instance, do you nibble to tide yourself over to a later-than-usual mealtime? ________

____

—Have you changed your place of eating? ________

____

—What activities do you now refrain from while eating? ________________________________

____

4. Take a look at how you have modified the eating process.
   a. Are you swallowing each forkful before adding more food to your fork? ________________
   b. Have you increased your eating time? ________
   c. Have you incorporated a two-minute delay into your meal? ________________________
   d. Are you enjoying your meals? Are you savoring your food? ________________________
5. Notice your changing attitude toward leftovers.
   a. Are you trying creative combinations of leftovers? ____
   b. Do you throw unusable food away? ________
   c. Did you send money to an organization that helps the needy or give money or food to a local project?

   ____
6. Do you consciously think about Christ's self-discipline when you are confronted with the desire to eat? ________
   a. What is your source of power for change in your lifestyle (Philippians 4:13)? ____________

   ____

b. How does your relationship with God relate to the effectiveness of His power in your life? ____________

____

____

c. Review and paraphrase Titus 2:11–13. ____________

____

____

7. Reflect on the last three weeks. What activities have you used to break an eating chain or delay eating? ________

____

____

8. How have you reminded yourself this week of your value in God's eyes? ____________________

____

9. Your reactions reflect your degree of control. Answer the following questions. Imagine each situation.

a. You and your spouse or friend come home from the movies. The other person dishes up ice cream for a bedtime snack and sits down to talk. What do you do?

____

____

b. You are at a covered-dish supper. After the main course everyone goes to the dessert table, choosing several desserts per person. How many different items do you put on your plate? ____________________

c. Everyone in the family has an activity to rush to after Thursday's dinner. You have a half hour to eat, clean up, and start out the door.

—Do you sit back, take a drink of water, and eat slowly, thinking, "I'll eat what time allows"? ________

—Do you join the family in gobbling down your food, afraid you won't get enough to eat to last you through the evening? ________________________________

d. As you clear the breakfast dishes, what do you do with the two bites of cinnamon toast left on a plate? ______

10. You are in the process of change and need to look continually for strategies that will encourage you. Look in the mirror. Would you like to change your hairstyle or buy one new dress that is truly flattering? How are you going to encourage yourself this week? ______________

____

11. Consider ways to make your new eating style seem like a change for the better. For instance, make eating special for you and your family with a simple bouquet of flowers or dinner music or your best china. Let a beautiful dinner atmosphere reflect the specialness of your new lifestyle. It will make other family members feel special too!

12. Think up new ways to remind yourself of the eating strategies for weight loss you have learned. You might change places with someone at the dinner table; it will give you a new perspective! ________________________

____

____

13. List some good-tasting low-calorie foods you can have within easy reach when you choose to eat a snack. Have

these foods ready to eat. An unpeeled, uncut carrot is no competition for an easy-to-grab cookie! ______________

____

____

Seek and Share

1. Discuss your long and short-term goals in self-discipline and weight reduction.
2. Take time now to record your personal goals and to make an honest evaluation of your progress.

____

____

____

____

3. Separate from the group with your prayer partner. Share your reflections on the question above and pray about your goals together.

   Read together and pray through Philippians 3:12–13.

9

DO NOT BE LED ASTRAY: SOCIAL PRESSURE TO EAT

Gwen is a legal assistant who works from nine to five. Wednesday was an especially busy day. After work she bolted to her aerobic dance class which she just began at the YWCA. She then headed across town for a 7:30 Business and Professional Women's committee meeting.

As she drove to the meeting, Gwen was feeling really good about herself. She had lost four pounds in the last month by cutting out substantial evening snacking. Aerobic dancing not only used up calories, but also made her feel good physically. She could sense her body getting into shape in only one month's time. This motivated her to continue this regimen.

Upon arriving, she chatted with her friends as her hostess served coffee and a deep-dish apple pie. Gwen consciously said to herself, "I'll just have coffee." Noticing that Gwen did not take dessert, her hostess said in a very pleasant and sincere voice, "Oh, Gwen, won't you have some pie? It is such a pleasure to bake for others to enjoy."

Gwen felt compelled to eat the dessert out of courtesy. Did she have any options?

The Influence of Others

1. What effect do others' habits and influences have over us (Proverbs 22:25)? ______________________

____

2. Read 2 Chronicles 22:3. Who encouraged Ahaziah to do wrong? ______________________

3. Read the account of John the Baptist's death (Matthew 14:3–9).

   —Who influenced Herodias's daughter (v. 8)? __________

   —Why did Herod's niece have such a devastating influence over him (v. 9)? ______________________

   ____

4. Who urged Abram to wrongly fulfill God's promise for children by sleeping with Hagar (Genesis 16:1–4)?

   ____

5. From the above illustrations, what can you conclude about the influence of those closest to us and the ones we love the most? ______________________

   ____

   Please keep in mind that these people can have the most *positive* influence too.

6. Who in your life has great influence over your eating?

   ____

____

____

7. How can you encourage these people to support you in your new eating lifestyle?

____

____

____

____

8. What should you do if your loved one brings home cream-filled doughnuts "just for you"?

____

____

Responding in Love

1. How should we respond to those from whom we refuse food (1 Peter 2:17)? ____________________

____

2. How might you honor your hostess/friend/relative without accepting more food?

____

____

____

____

3. If you announce, "Oh, I'm on a diet" to someone who has just lovingly prepared a dinner for you, what might be your hostess's unspoken response? _______________

____

4. What can a "simple boast" produce (James 3:5)?

____

5. What can we expect after a "prideful moment" (Proverbs 16:18)? ______________________________

____

6. How do you feel when someone constantly talks about her diet? ______________________________

____

7. Put Psalm 44:8 into your own words. ______________

____

____

8. If you are *quietly,* before God, changing your eating lifestyle, in whom shall you boast? ______________

____

Strategy for Social Occasions

It is important to have a game plan. As you dress for a social occasion, implant in your mind your strategy for the evening. Suggestions:

1. Place yourself far away from the hors d'oeuvres. As you chat, work yourself to the opposite side of the room. Speak to at least one or two people before getting to the food.

2. Beverages can contain many hidden calories. Choose low-calorie drinks *when they are offered.* Sip others slowly. Even one alcoholic drink can alter your eating style. Try to avoid all influences that weaken your conviction not to overeat.

3. Memorize several responses you can give to refuse more food, yet sincerely compliment your host or hostess.
4. Consider several topics of conversation you especially want to address to your host or hostess. Immediately after politely refusing food, bring up one of those topics.
5. If you are attending a social occasion with a loved one, arrange a hidden or silent signal (a wink or gentle squeeze) to remind you not to eat. For instance, if you are about to go back for seconds at a buffet, your husband can give you a hidden reminder, and then you can choose your own course of action. Remind your supporters never to verbalize reminders in public.
6. Review in your mind strategies you have put into practice, such as eating slowly.
7. Take several inconspicuous deep breaths as you survey and make mental selections from the array of food on the buffet table. During this time, remind yourself of your intentions. You may have just a couple of seconds between conversations to do this, yet it will heighten your awareness and give you time to plan your selection.

Restaurant Eating: The Lion's Den

1. Before you go, *plan*. Ask yourself:

   —Are you going to eat bread or rolls while waiting for your entree?

   —What is your game plan for the salad bar? How many scoops of dressing will you use? What about croutons or other non-vegetable items? If your salad is served, ask for the dressing on the side so *you* can control the amount.

   —What will your side orders be? Suggestions:

   –Avoid French fries.

–Order baked potato with butter or sour cream on the *side*.

–Consider ordering all low-calorie vegetables.

—What are your dessert options?

–How about fresh fruit from the appetizer list (check it out while you make your menu selection)?

–Sherbet is usually available, but sometimes not mentioned. Ask for it.

–When appropriate, try to give your dessert selection first. This decreases your chance of being influenced by others' high-calorie orders.

–Enjoy some coffee or tea.

2. Be politely assertive by:

   —asking for frequent water refills.

   —being honest with your waitress if she is hurrying you.

   —asking that rolls and hors d'oeuvres not be brought to the table. If you have decided against dessert, ask that the dessert cart not be brought to the table. These suggestions are appropriate only if you are eating with a supporter who agrees to the suggestion beforehand.

3. Remember, your weight reduction strategies are personal. Try not to inconvenience others who are with you. Consider your company first, yet do not necessarily follow their example.

Holiday Eating

1. How do your eating habits change over the holiday seasons? ______________________________

   ____

   ____

Why? ____________________

____

Describe your childhood holiday experiences relating to food. ____________________

____

____

2. If you tend to overeat at holiday meals in a parent's home, reverse the invitation. When entertaining in your own home, you have control of the menu and your own serving portions.
3. Preparing for holiday celebrations can be a very joyous time. Tradition runs deep. List the foods you always prepare for Christmas (special cookies, fruitcake, candy, etc.):

____________	____________
____________	____________
____________	____________
____________	____________
____________	____________
____________	____________
____________	____________
____________	____________

a. Why do you prepare these items? ____________________

____

____

b. Who eats them? ____________________

c. Do you give them away as gifts? ____________________

d. When are these items served? ____________________

____

4. What is usually served at the family meal celebration? __

____

____

____

5. What is absolutely essential to make holidays festive? Make a "game plan" for food preparation for next year.

Foods you will make for next Christmas	Food items you will eliminate next Christmas
____________________	____________________
____________________	____________________
____________________	____________________
____________________	____________________

6. List new ways (other than food) that you can make the Christmas holidays festive and meaningful. ____________

____

____

____

To Do This Week

1. Consider your practices, traditions, and eating habits at other holidays: Easter, Mother's Day, the Fourth of July, Thanksgiving, birthdays.

____

____

____

2. How can you change these without losing the spirit of celebration?

Memorize and implant in your heart 1 John 3:7a: "Dear children, do not let anyone lead you astray."

Seek and Share

1. List situations in which you have experienced pressure to eat. Identify camouflaged influences to eat more than you want. Consider social situations, family and friend relationships, restaurant eating, and church functions. ___

2. Evaluate situations in which you may be exerting pressure to eat on others. ___

   How does the saying "misery loves company" relate to pressures to eat? ___

3. Plan a luncheon this week, with each class member bringing a favorite dish (making sure you have a nutritionally balanced meal). Do this for fellowship and the opportunity to practice concepts learned this week.

10

STRESSED OUT, BULGING OUT

Headaches, insomnia, irritability, diarrhea, strained relationships, excessive drinking, and *overeating* are just a few of the possible negative responses to stress in our lives. We may not be able to change life's circumstances, but we can change our perception of them, and ultimately our response. In other words, it is not necessary to respond to a marital tiff with fifteen Oreo cookies and a tall glass of milk!

Unplanned, excess eating can occur in any number of stress-filled situations:

—Studying for an exam
—After an argument
—When you are dissatisfied with your job
—When you are lonely
—When you are hurt or angry
—In the midst of a terribly busy day
—When you are tired

As Christians, we have a source of calm that goes beyond every book on stress, every stress-release technique—Christ's calming and redirective hands. God sums up His answer to our need when He says, "Be still and know that I am God" (Psalm 46:10).

Read Proverbs 24:32 and prepare your heart to reflect on areas of stress in your life. (Record notes here.) ____________

____

Martha's Bad Day

Turn to Luke 10:38–41. Place yourself in Martha's shoes.

1. What would you think and do if a loved one and his friends dropped in unexpectedly for lunch? ____________

   ____

   ____

2. Why was Martha feeling stress and what was her response? ______________________________

   ____

3. What does Jesus say she is worried and upset about (vs. 41)? ______________________________________

   ____

4. How does Martha's experience apply to your daily life? _

   ____

Seeking the Right Perspective

1. What is God *not* the author of (1 Corinthians 14:33)?

   ____

2. As you read Galatians 5:7–9, describe how we can so easily lose perspective of our life events. ____________

____

____

3. Martha needed to choose between the many details of being a fine hostess and listening to Jesus. Her choice was between something of immediate earthly value and matters of eternal consequence.

   —List those things in your daily living which you constantly struggle to accomplish (those "I must do" thoughts which circulate in your mind all day).

   ____________________ ____________________

   ____________________ ____________________

   ____________________ ____________________

   ____________________ ____________________

   ____________________ ____________________

   ____________________ ____________________

   —List the activities and/or important factors in your life which are of ultimate value to you.

   ____________________ ____________________

   ____________________ ____________________

   ____________________ ____________________

   ____________________ ____________________

   ____________________ ____________________

   ____________________ ____________________

4. Read Luke 12:34. How can distinguishing between those things of true personal importance and those of only temporary value affect your perspective on potentially stress-filled situations? ____________________

____

____

5. Experts on stress say how we perceive situations will determine our response. How can the knowledge of Christ and the elements of Christian living affect both our *perspective* and *response*? _______________

____

____

Out of Control

Feeling out of control of life's circumstances or events of daily living is a known source of stress.

1. What, in your life, do you feel lack of control in? _______________

____

____

____

Take some time and seriously evaluate your daily living habits and structure.

2. How might you add to or subtract from your activities and goals to feel more "in control"? _______________

____

3. Eating in response to stress causes *additional stress.* A cycle of "stress upon stress" occurs. (See chart on page 99.)

4. In what stress-filled circumstances do you respond by overeating? _______________

____

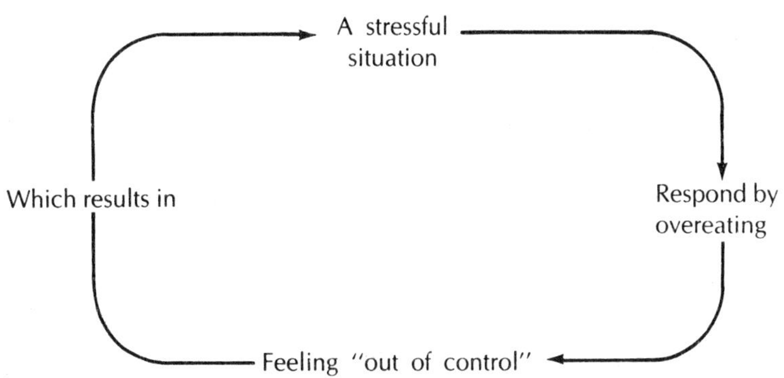

5. Do you eat to delay a phone call you really don't want to make or a chore you don't want to do? ________

Innovative Stress Release: Positive Response to Pressure

PRAYER

1. What is our ultimate privilege as we seek relief from stress (Hebrews 4:16)? ________

   ____

2. What are we to communicate to God (Psalm 62:8)?

   ____

3. What should we do in times of anxiety (Philippians 4:6–7)? ________

   ____

4. How should we pray (1 Thessalonians 5:17)? ________

   ____

5. What are we assured of (1 John 5:14)? ______________________

____

GOD'S WORD

1. What does God's Word provide?

   James 1:5 ______________________________

   Matthew 11:28 ___________________________

   Psalm 119:24 ____________________________

   Psalm 119:28 ____________________________

   Psalm 119:37 ____________________________

   Psalm 119:45 ____________________________

   Psalm 119:52 ____________________________

2. What perspective does God's Word give us (Psalm 119:89)? ______________________________

   ____

EXERCISE

Most scientists agree that exercise is a natural stress reliever. It has also proven to be good therapy for depression. In addition, exercise strengthens the bones, controls weight, and can be fun (believe it or not!). So why don't most Americans exercise? Surveys reveal three main reasons. Check any of these that apply to you.

___People feel they have no time in their busy schedules.
___They are too tired to exercise.
___They think their daily routines provide adequate exercise.

Perhaps your lack of scheduled exercise reveals its position on your scale of priorities. If you place exercise in the same league as brushing your teeth—essential for body maintenance—your daily schedule may need to change. Outline your typical day on page 103.

1. How can you rearrange your day to allow for exercise time? ______________________________

____

2. What are you willing to sacrifice in order to exercise? ____

____

3. If you feel too tired to exercise, perhaps you are in a common vicious cycle:

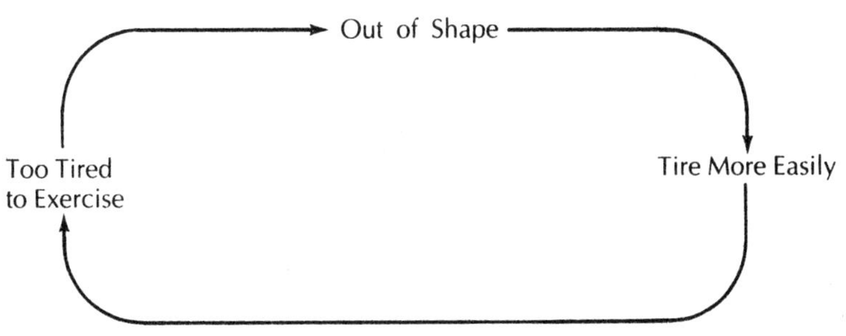

   People who exercise regularly claim to have more energy and feel less tired than before they began exercising. Sporadic exercise, however, or the initial stages of regular exercise, may cause fatigue. Are you willing to persevere long enough to overcome this? ____

4. If you feel you get enough exercise raking the lawn and cleaning house, ask yourself these questions:

   a. Do you exercise three or four times a week? ________

   b. Do you exercise for twenty to thirty minutes each time? ______________________________

c. Is it aerobic exercise, which strengthens your heart and lungs? ______________________
(Aerobic exercise causes your heart to pump vigorously and requires your body to use more oxygen.)

Aerobic Exercises (Nonstop Rhythmic Activities)

running	cross-country skiing
brisk walking	jumping rope
swimming	aerobic dancing
bike riding	stationary cycling or running
basketball	handball
soccer	squash
racquetball	fast-paced tennis

Non-Aerobic Exercises (Stop-and-Go Activities)

tennis (doubles)	sprinting
downhill skiing	isometrics
football	square dancing
calisthenics	golf
weight lifting	

5. Here are some pointers for starting an exercise program.

a. Consult your physician before beginning an exercise routine.

b. Choose an aerobic exercise you enjoy.

c. Use good equipment to prevent accidents or physical injury (i.e., running shoes for running, eye guards for racquetball).

A.M.	*Activity*
6	
7	
8	
9	
10	
11	
12	

P.M.	
1	
2	
3	
4	
5	
6	
7	
8	
9	
10	
11	

d. Try not to let a bad day discourage you. Everyone has good and bad days of exercise.

e. Make lifestyle changes that will give you additional exercise.

—Walk briskly or bike to work if possible.

—Take stairs instead of elevators.

—Park your car at the far end of the parking lot.

—Jump rope during commercials of a favorite TV show.

REST

Fatigue is also a form of stress. We often try to relieve it by eating. We look for food to restore our energy, when what we really need is sleep. When we are tired, our willpower to abstain from food is diminished.

Do you eat more at the end of the day, when you are tired?

____

Have you found it hard to practice eating lifestyle changes when you have been unusually tired? ____________________

If you are tired, but feel you must stay awake, what do you do? ______________________________________

Exercise actually relieves fatigue on a short-term basis. It restores energy. When you are very tired, but must accomplish one more hour of work before "hitting the sack," five or ten minutes of exercise can revitalize you and take the place of eating. What exercise will you plan to do?

____

GOOD NUTRITION

1. Eating breakfast improves your health, your learning ability, and your concentration. Remember, when you get up you have gone ten or twelve hours without food.

Avoid excess sodium.

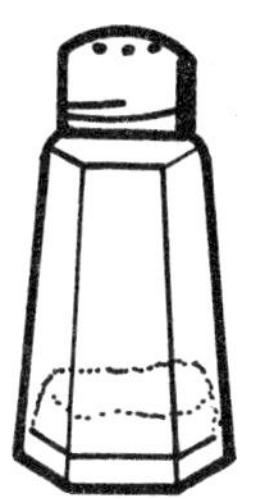

- Learn to enjoy unsalted flavors by using more herbs and spices.
- Cook with small amounts of salt or none at all.
- Keep the salt shaker off the table.
- Limit salty foods such as potato chips, pretzels, corn chips, condiments (soy sauce, steak sauce, seasoned salts), pickled foods, ham, bacon and other cured meats.

Limit your total fat intake, saturated fat and cholesterol.

- Choose lean meat, fish, poultry, dry beans, and peas as your protein source (trim off any visible fat).
- Moderate your use of eggs and of cheese made with whole milk (except children).
- Use soft margarines instead of butter, lard, hard-stick margarines, shortening, and coconut oil (such as non-dairy creamers and whipped toppings).
- When you must use oil, use vegetable oils such as corn, safflower and sunflower.
- Substitute non-fat and low-fat milk for whole milk (except children).
- Avoid frying; instead broil, bake, or steam items.

Avoid excess sugars.

• Use less sugars, including white sugar, brown sugar, raw sugar, honey, and syrups.

• Avoid candy, soft drinks, ice cream, cakes, and cookies.

• Select fresh fruits or fruits canned without sugar or syrup.

• Read labels. If the term sucrose, glucose, maltose, dextrose, lactose, fructose, or syrups appear first, there is a large percentage of sugar. Remember, if the word ends in "ose" it is probably a sugar.

Increase fiber intake.

• Eat whole grain cereals and breads (read labels carefully to avoid breads brown in color, yet low in whole grain).

• Substitute highly refined items such as white rice, noodles, and macaroni with whole grain items.

2. Food choices based on moderation and variety promote better health.

3. Regular mealtimes also decrease stress.

PERSONAL COMMITMENT

1. Do you read Scripture and pray daily? ________________

2. When that "stressed out" feeling occurs, do you seek God? ________________________________
   How? ________________________________

   ____

3. If you do not already have a quiet time before the Lord each day, are you willing to begin having one? ________

   ____

   To whom will you be accountable in this new lifestyle change? ____________________________

4. Choose a Scripture verse about peace (good ones are Isaiah 26:3; Psalm 119:165; John 14:27; Philippians 4:7; Colossians 3:15). Write it on a three-by-five card and place it in a convenient spot. Commit yourself to meditate on it when you feel stressed and pressured.

5. Make contact with your prayer partner this week, sharing Scripture and praying over your individual responses to stress.

6. If you already exercise regularly, what do you do? ______
   Is it aerobic? ____________________________
   If you do not do regular aerobic exercise, make a game plan to help you start.

   —What activity will you choose? ________________

   —What day will you start? ____________________

   —When during the day will you exercise? __________

   —If your activity requires a partner, with whom will you do it? ______________________________

   —To whom will you be accountable? ______________

7. Do you get six to eight hours of sleep a night? ________

   If not, will you rearrange your schedule to do so?

   ____

8. Do you eat breakfast? __________________________

   Do you eat well-balanced meals? ________________

What changes do you need to make? ________________

____

9. Who is your source of all comfort (2 Corinthians 1:3–4)?

____

To Do This Week

At the end of each day, reflect on the day's events and your responses to them. Record on page 109 any time you ate as a response to stress. Or make your own chart, if that one isn't big enough. (Remember, boredom is also a stressor!)

Seek and Share

1. Bring a recipe or food preparation idea that supports the nutrition guidelines on pages 105–106. (For example: a low-sodium supper idea.)
2. Discuss ways to motivate yourself to exercise. Set individual, realistic goals. (For example: a brisk ten-minute walk.)

For further study. The following are recommended for more in-depth reading on stress, exercise, and nutrition.

1. *Stress/Unstress,* Keith W. Schnert, Augsburg Publishing House, 1981.

2. *Jane Brody's Nutrition Book,* Jane Brody, Norton Publishing, 1981.

3. *The New Aerobics,* Kenneth H. Cooper, New York: Bantam, 1970.

	Event	Approximate Time	Responded by Eating (Write Food/Amount)
Mon.			
Tue.			
Wed.			
Thur.			
Fri.			
Sat.			
Sun.			

11

THE MIND GAP

A deli sandwich: thoughts of roast beef, tomatoes, lettuce, onion, spices, and hot pepper invade your mind. Although you have an hour before lunch, your body reacts to your mind cue with feelings of hunger. Our minds are indeed the source of our desires and actions.

But we can interpret the same information several different ways. Our interpretation will affect our behavior. (See diagram next page.)

The same situation or stimulus can lead to either behavior response, depending on how we interpret it. One response will contribute to your new, disciplined lifestyle; the other will not.

David exhorted his son Solomon to serve God with wholehearted devotion and with a *willing mind* (1 Chronicles 28:9). Changed thought patterns take just such a mind—a mind obedient to Christ and willing to use His resources.

Interpretation Alternatives

1. At the ice cream parlor, you are deciding whether to have one or two scoops.

2A. "Mint chocolate is so good, I'd better have two scoops."

2B. "One scoop will be a real treat. It will give me a chance to savor that delicious mint chocolate."

Changing Thought Patterns

1. Read Psalm 94:11. Who knows our thoughts? ________
   What kind of thoughts do we have? ________

   ____

2. Write Isaiah 65:2 in your own words: ________

   ____

   ____

3. Describe how your thoughts can work against your goal of weight loss. ________

   ____

As you attempt to suppress thoughts of eating, what actually happens? ____________________

____

4. Only when thoughts are *redirected,* not suppressed, can you begin to control your thought patterns.

   —Read 2 Corinthians 10:5. Do we make our thoughts obedient to Christ passively or actively? __________ Who takes the initiative? __________

   —Write any special Scripture verse which you have implanted in your mind and heart. __________

   ____

   This will be your key thought diversion when for no reason your mind says "Eat."

   —Changing your activity usually redirects your mind. Write three five-minute activities which you need to accomplish.

   __________ __________

   ____

   When you realize you are concentrating on a dangerous thought, you can do one of these diversion activities.

Exploring Your Mindset

1. As a group, consider each of the following negative thoughts. (Do you ever experience the thought?) Write a positive, constructive thought that could redirect your mindset, as in the example.

Negative Thought	*Constructive Thought*
—I binged terribly this afternoon. I blew it again. I might as well forget trying for the day!	I binged terribly this afternoon. What's done is done. Now let me think, what influenced me to do it? What will be my game plan to avoid overeating again?

Negative Thought	*Constructive Thought*
—I really feel guilty for eating that homemade pie at Janet's.	
—It's the weekend; I'll just blow my diet.	
—I feel so deprived on this diet.	
—I'd better eat this now; I may not have a chance later.	
—I have to eat everything I ordered in the restaurant. This is a treat, and besides, I'm paying for it.	

2. Changing your "self-dialogue" takes time. Improvement will be gradual. Share with your prayer partner one occasion when you diverted a potential negative thought into positive and realistic thinking.

Using Imagery

1. When I am trying to muster up steam to get up the first neighborhood hill on a morning jog, I think about a lovely, expensive brown wool suit I bought during skinnier days. The lining is now split by the stress of a few extra pounds and I look very unbecoming in it. Visualizing that suit and thinking about how I feel when trying it on motivates me to reach the top of the hill.

   Other examples of imagery include remembering how good you felt about yourself the two days last week that you refrained from evening eating; or imagining every detail about an upcoming party—people, food, clothes, conversation; then imagining what you will eat, where you will stand, and how you will respond to tempting situations; or imagining feeling fast and sleek on a tennis court.

2. Write down an image you can use to help solve a personal problem area of eating. ____________________

   ____

   ____

3. Imagery is also helpful in increasing spiritual awareness.

   a. Paraphrase Psalm 119:15: ____________________

   ____

	Biblical Experience	Personal Experience with God
God's Faithfulness		
Christ's Forthright Love		
The Holy Spirit's Guidance		

b. Fill in examples of imagery for the following:

c. Is there a problem area in your life that biblically based imagery could help? What image would you use? ____

____

Prayer: The Steel Girder Behind Changed Thoughts

Take some time for personal evaluation as you consider prayer's role in changing thought patterns.

1. Why is it important to back our strategies for change by prayer (Philippians 3:3)? ______

   ______

   Have you been relying on personal (fleshly) striving, alone? ______

2. What does faith have to do with prayer (Matthew 17:20)?

   ______

   ______

   What is your heartfelt attitude when you approach God about changing your thoughts? With what degree of faith do you come before Him? ______

3. Honesty with God

   Read Psalm 142:1–2. How does David tell God of his troubles? ______

   ______

   How honest are you in bringing your destructive thought patterns to God? Do you lay them all out before Him, or do you partially suppress them? ______

   ______

4. How will God honor your prayer (Luke 11:9–13)?

   ______

   ______

5. What do we believers have (1 Corinthians 2:16)? ______

   ______

Negative By-Products of a Challenge

1. What do you do when you feel frustrated in the weight loss process? ______

Read Psalm 26:3 and Psalm 29:11. What is God's promise to you in times of utter frustration? ____________

____

____

2. Have you felt a sense of failure or defeat at any time during this Bible study? ______________________

   Read Psalm 40:2–3. How does it make you feel? ______

   ____

3. Have your goals for weight loss and lifestyle change been realistic? Or are you defeated by inappropriate expectations? ________________________________

   ____

   Do you allow yourself small and occasional setbacks without excessive self-criticism? ______________

   ____

   What are your goals now that this study is almost over?

   ____

   ____

   ____

An Encouraging Word

As you seek to change your mindset, be encouraged by Amos 4:13:

"He who forms the mountains,
 creates the wind,
 and reveals his thoughts to man,

he who turns dawn to darkness,
and treads the high places of the earth—
The LORD God Almighty is his name."

Seek and Share

1. Read 1 Timothy 4:8. Discuss what perspective we should have as we strive for weight loss.
2. With your prayer partner, focus on your needs for thought-change in eating. Read together 1 Samuel 12:23.

To Do This Week

Keep a week's journal of prayer specifically focused toward changed thought patterns.

12

PRESSING FORWARD

Bad habits go away slowly, don't they? No doubt you have experienced both peaks and valleys in striving for lifestyle change. Yet as bad habits weaken and wither, positive habits find room to grow and flourish.

Each small success is a steppingstone to a fuller life of self-control. Permanent change, not over weeks or months, but over years and decades, is our goal.

As you seek to maintain your new lifestyle, beware. Strategies may grow old; loved ones may fail you; old habits may try to spring up. Only God's steadfastness is unchangeable. It is the *only* resource in this whole endeavor which does not fluctuate.

God has a vested interest in our desires and struggles. And although our minds and will change, "God is not a man . . . that he should change his mind" (Numbers 23:19).

Although this study is coming to a close, let's evaluate the course you are on and your present commitment to continue. The changes you have incorporated into your lifestyle need to continue in order to grow strong.

1. Read Proverbs 20:25. What is your level of commitment to continue reducing your weight through lifestyle change? ____

   ____

2. Check each strategy you have continued throughout this study.

   ___Placing utensil down between bites.

   ___Savoring food.

   ___Slowing your eating time.

   ___Eating only in designated areas.

   ___Eating and only eating.

   ___Considering Christ's discipline as you seek self-control in specific situations.

   ___Breaking eating chains by doing alternate activities.

   ___Delaying eating by setting a timer.

   ___Adhering to a game plan in a restaurant.

   ___Diverting conversation when offered food in social situations.

3. Has your image of yourself changed since chapter 1? If so, how? ____

   ____

   ____

4. Do you recognize stress in your life and work at finding positive ways to relieve it? Do you consciously avoid

eating when uptight? ____

____

____

5. When you feel pulled back toward a bad habit or trapped in that habit, what will God do (Psalm 25:15)? __

   ____

6. Using the image of fruit, what does Jesus say about self-control (John 15:5)? ____

   ____

7. What is a man without self-control compared with (Proverbs 25:28)? ____

   ____

   ____

8. Put Psalm 73:26 into your own words. ____________________

   ____

   ____

9. What does God promise in our failures (Psalm 145:14)? _

   ____

10. As children of God, what are we urged to do (1 Thessalonians 5:8)? ____

    ____

    ____

11. What does God promise in every human endeavor we bring to Him (Jeremiah 29:11)? __________________________

    ____

Although Proverbs 11:1 refers to integrity in the marketplace, you might enjoy reading it with weight control in mind.

> "The Lord abhors dishonest scales, but accurate weights are his delight"!

Seek and Share

1. Make plans for a get-together in one month to fellowship together and encourage one another. Plan to be accountable to one another for your progress throughout the month.
2. Consider whether you want to continue meeting as a group for support in your ongoing endeavor for weight control.
3. Share which strategies in this Bible study were most helpful to you. Why? Share one strategy you want to strengthen this month.
4. Pray together for continued motivation and protection from old habits.